P9-BZM-588

Who Was
Helen Keller?

by Gare Thompson

illustrated by Nancy Harrison

Penguin Workshop

To my mother, Irene Pine—GT

PENGUIN WORKSHOP
An Imprint of Penguin Random House LLC, New York

Text copyright © 2003 by Gare Thompson.
Illustrations copyright © 2003 by Nancy Harrison.
Cover illustration copyright © 2003 by Penguin Random House LLC. All rights reserved.
Published by Penguin Workshop, an imprint of Penguin Random House LLC, New York.
PENGUIN and PENGUIN WORKSHOP are trademarks of Penguin Books Ltd.
WHO HQ & Design is a registered trademark of Penguin Random House LLC.
Printed in the USA.

Visit us online at www.penguinrandomhouse.com.

Library of Congress Control Number: 2003017972

ISBN 9780448431444

Contents

Who Was
Helen Keller?

Born more than 100 years ago, Helen learned to speak and read and write. Those may not sound like great accomplishments. But Helen Keller was both deaf and blind.

HELEN KELLER

Imagine that your ears are stuffed with cotton. You can't hear anything—not even someone shouting. A blindfold covers your eyes. You can't see anything, either. Your world is dark and silent. This was Helen Keller's world.

When Helen grew up, few deaf people learned how to speak. There were very few schools for deaf and blind children. Few blind people learned how to read and write. Helen Keller not only did both, but also did much more. She wrote several best-selling books. And she gave lectures around the world. She showed that her handicaps had not held her back. Above all, she gave hope to other people who, like her, could not hear or see.

Chapter 1
The Early Years

Helen Keller was born on June 27, 1880, in Tuscumbia, Alabama. Her father, Arthur Keller, had fought in the Civil War for the South. After the war, he went home to his farm. After his first wife died, and he married a woman named Kate Adams. His two sons from his first marriage and

CAPTAIN KELLER

KATE KELLER

his young wife called Arthur Keller, "Captain." In addition to running his farm, Captain was also the editor of the local paper. He was a quiet, stern man.

The first girl in the family, baby Helen lit up a room. She laughed and cooed. Helen was the apple

KELLER HOME IN TUSCUMBIA

of her mother's eye. Her father adored her. Helen wrote about her early life. She said, "The beginning of my life was simple and much like every other little life . . . I came, I saw, I conquered, as the first baby in the family always does."

Helen was smart. She spoke early. Her first words were said to be "tea, tea, tea" and "wah-wah" for water. If she did not know the words for things, Helen made up signals to show her mother what she wanted. She learned to walk at an early age. Soon Helen was racing around the house.

Then before she was two years old, Helen became sick. Very sick. She ran a very high fever. At that time, there were few medicines to cure sickness. The doctor thought that Helen would

die. Then, suddenly, the fever broke. Helen slept peacefully. Her family rejoiced. Their golden daughter was fine again.

But Helen wasn't fine. While Helen's mother was bathing her, she moved her hand in front of Helen's face. Helen did not blink. Helen's eyes stared straight ahead. Kate tried again. She hoped that she was wrong. But she wasn't. Helen was blind. And that was not all.

Every evening, a bell was rung to call the family to dinner. Everyone heard the loud, clanging noise. They stopped what they were doing and came to dinner. But Kate noticed that Helen no longer turned her head toward the sound. Kate called to the Captain and his sister Evelyn, who lived with

them. They shouted at Helen. They spoke softly. They clapped their hands next to her ears. Helen did not react. Mrs. Keller's fear was true. Her daughter was deaf as well as blind.

Her parents took Helen to a doctor. The doctor checked her, but there was nothing he could do. *How,* Mrs. Keller wondered, *would her smart, beautiful little girl learn to live in her silent, dark world?*

Chapter 2
Dark Years

There were no days or nights in Helen's world. She could not see the sun rising each morning or the moon with its silver glow at night. She could not hear birds sing or crickets chirp. She lived in silent darkness. Imagine if you could not hear, see,

or speak. How would you let people understand you? How would you "talk"?

Helen was smart. She followed her mother around everywhere. She clung to her skirts.

Helen noticed different smells. She felt vibrations as people and things moved around her. Over time, Helen found ways to communicate. She made up signals to tell people what she wanted.

There were not many schools for deaf or blind children when Helen was little. There were none where she lived in Alabama. At schools for the deaf, children learned to make signs with their hands. The signs stood for words.

By the time she turned five, Helen had made up over fifty signs of her own. She pulled at her mother or her father. That meant "come with me."

SIGN LANGUAGE

LONG AGO, A GROUP OF DEAF PEOPLE IN PARIS, FRANCE, DEVELOPED THEIR OWN SIGN LANGUAGE. THEN, IN 1755, A TEACHER WHO COULD HEAR, ABBÉ CHARLES MICHEL DE L'EPÉE, LEARNED THESE SIGNS AND ADDED NEW ONES TO FORM A STANDARD SIGN LANGUAGE OF FRENCH. NOW HEARING AND NON-HEARING PEOPLE COULD COMMUNICATE! MANY OF THE FRENCH SIGNS FROM LONG AGO ARE STILL USED TODAY.

She shoved them away when she wanted them to go. For "bread," Helen acted out cutting a slice and buttering it. To say "small," Helen pinched a small bit of the skin of her hand. Helen spread her fingers wide and brought them together to mean "large." Helen also had signs for everyone in her family. For Captain, or Father, Helen mimed glasses

and for her mother, she pulled her hair into a knot at the back of her head.

The family tried to understand Helen, but it was not easy. She had a terrible temper. When Helen did not get her way, she threw a tantrum.

Helen knew that people talked with their lips. She tried moving her lips, but no sounds came out. She did not understand why. It made Helen so mad. She kicked and screamed with frustration. Her tantrums stopped only after she became too tired to scream anymore.

Helen's parents did not know how to handle her. Relatives told them that Helen should no longer live at home. She should be "put away." That meant putting Helen in a hospital or home for the blind and deaf. In the nineteenth century, people with handicaps were often sent away like this. Once they were sent away, their family often did not see them again. But Mrs. Keller did not want to do that to her daughter. She knew her daughter was smart. But how could anyone teach her?

Chapter 3
Helen Teaches Herself

Even in her dark world, Helen had happy times. She loved to be outdoors. She'd feel her way carefully along the walls of the house. Helen loved to touch all the plants that grew around the house. She smelled the flowers. Soon she could tell plants apart by their feel and smell. This was how she got information.

Helen learned to do simple chores. She folded the clean clothes. She knew which clothes were hers. She also learned that when her

mother put on her coat, she was going out. Helen tugged at her coat to go, too.

But for Helen everyday mishaps could turn into dangerous accidents. Once Helen spilled some water on her apron. She wanted it to dry. So she held her apron near the fireplace. She did not know how close she was to the fire. Her apron

burst into flames. Quickly, her nurse used a blanket to put out the fire. It burned only Helen's fingers slightly and singed her hair. Helen had been very lucky.

As she grew older, Helen developed a sense of mischief. She liked to play tricks. One day, Helen found some keys. She knew that keys locked doors. Her mother was in the pantry getting something, and Helen was right outside. Helen took the keys and locked her mother in the pantry. Her mother pounded on the door. She yelled to be let out. Helen sat on the porch where she could feel the vibrations of her mother's pounding. Helen sat there and smiled. Mrs. Keller was locked in the pantry for three hours.

Helen and a young servant named Martha
Washington often played together. Martha was a
few years older than Helen. But Helen was the
bossier of the two. One day, they were cutting out
paper dolls on the porch. Helen soon grew tired of
this. So she cut off all the flowers growing on vines
near the porch. Still bored, Helen decided to cut
Martha's hair. Martha said no at first, but then
gave in. Few people said no to Helen. So Martha's
hair soon lay at her feet. And, then, because she felt

that it was only fair, Helen let Martha cut her own long, golden hair. Helen's mother was not happy with either child.

Helen's other friend was the family dog, Belle. Helen tried to teach the dog her signs. But the dog would just sleep or run off after a bird. Helen could not understand why Belle was such a poor student.

And so Helen passed her days.

Then, when Helen was five, her sister Mildred was born. Suddenly Helen's world changed. Someone else needed her mother's love. Someone else sat in her mother's lap. Helen became jealous of the baby who seemed to be taking her mother away.

One day, Helen discovered her baby sister sleeping in her doll's cradle. Helen grew very angry. Before anyone else could stop her, Helen pushed over the cradle. Mildred tumbled out. Luckily, Mrs. Keller caught Mildred before she hit the floor. Now, Mrs. Keller realized that Helen was not only a danger to herself. She was a danger to others. If Helen's mother could not control Helen who was still a young girl, what would happen when Helen got older? Helen had to change.

The Kellers took Helen to another doctor in Baltimore, Maryland. The doctor was an eye specialist. Again the Kellers heard the same words. There was nothing the doctor could do for Helen. But the doctor did tell Captain Keller about Alexander Graham Bell who lived in nearby Washington, D.C. Bell, who had invented the telephone in 1876, was also a former teacher of the deaf. Perhaps Bell might know someone to help Helen.

For the first time in a very long while, the Kellers felt a little bit of hope.

ALEXANDER GRAHAM BELL

TODAY ALEXANDER GRAHAM BELL IS BEST KNOWN FOR INVENTING THE TELEPHONE. BUT HE ALSO WORKED ALL HIS LIFE TO HELP THE DEAF. HIS MOTHER WAS NEARLY DEAF. AS A YOUNG MAN, BELL TAUGHT DEAF CHILDREN. HE USED DRAWINGS TO TEACH THE DEAF HOW TO USE THEIR TONGUE, LIPS, AND VOCAL CHORDS TO SPEAK. ONE OF THE

DEAF STUDENTS HE WORKED WITH WAS MABEL HUBBARD. SHE HAD LOST HER HEARING AS A RESULT OF AN ILLNESS AS A YOUNG GIRL. A BRIGHT AND EAGER GIRL, SHE MADE GREAT PROGRESS. IN TIME, THE TWO FELL IN LOVE AND MARRIED. BELL'S WORK WITH SOUND AND SPEECH HELPED HIM TO CREATE THE TELEPHONE IN 1876.

Chapter 4
A Ray of Hope

Accompanied by the Captain and her Aunt Evelyn, Helen went to see Dr. Bell. Her mother carefully curled Helen's hair before she left. Helen looked like an angel. She was about six years old now.

Helen walked into Bell's office, and the two became friends right away. Helen got on Bell's lap. The young child and the inventor felt at home with each other. Helen later wrote in her autobiography, "He understood my signs, and I knew it and loved him at once." Bell felt that Helen could learn. He thought she was a smart and sensible girl. He wanted to see her succeed. Maybe, just maybe, Helen Keller could lead a more normal life.

Bell gave Helen his watch to play with as he talked to Captain. He told Captain to write to the Perkins Institution for the Blind in Boston, Massachusetts (later called Perkins School). Dr. Bell told Captain that forty years earlier a deaf-blind child, Laura Bridgman, had been taught to read, write, and talk with hand signals. He was sure that the Kellers could find a teacher for Helen there.

Once back at home, Captain wrote to the head of the Perkins School. Captain Keller wrote that he needed a teacher for his daughter. The Kellers waited anxiously for his reply.

Michael Anagnos, the head of Perkins, wrote back that he did have a teacher in mind. Her name was Anne Sullivan. The Kellers were thrilled. What they did not know was that Anne Sullivan still needed to be convinced to take the job.

Who was Anne Sullivan? Anne, or Annie as she was called, was an orphan who had had a very hard and lonely life. As a child, she had been partially blind.

She was sent to the Perkins School and later on, operations restored her sight. Annie graduated first in her class at Perkins. Like Helen Keller, she was very bright and also very stubborn.

ANNIE SULLIVAN

At twenty, Annie had never been a teacher. She was not sure she could do the job, or even that she wanted it. Mr. Anagnos kept encouraging her. He felt that this lonely, intelligent young woman would be right for the job. And Annie did not have many other choices open to her. It was either the teaching job or a job in a factory. Annie decided to take the job with the Kellers.

Annie took two months to prepare for her new job. She had met Laura Bridgman. She learned the manual alphabet. She talked to Laura by spelling into her hand. Now she studied the different ways to teach the manual alphabet. Annie prepared the best that she could. But really she had no idea what lay before her or how her new job would change her life.

THOMAS HOPKINS GALLAUDET

THOMAS HOPKINS GALLAUDET OF HARTFORD, CONNECTICUT, WAS THE MAN WHO BROUGHT EDUCATION TO DEAF CHILDREN IN AMERICA. HE WANTED TO HELP HIS NEIGHBOR'S YOUNG DEAF DAUGHTER, ALICE COGSWELL. IN 1816, GALLAUDET WENT TO PARIS, FRANCE, TO STUDY AT A SCHOOL FOR DEAF PEOPLE. AFTER A FEW MONTHS, HE RETURNED TO AMERICA, DETERMINED TO START HIS OWN SCHOOL. HE BROUGHT A FRENCH SIGN LANGUAGE TEACHER BACK WITH HIM. IN 1817, GALLAUDET FOUNDED THE NATION'S FIRST SCHOOL FOR DEAF PEOPLE IN HARTFORD, CONNECTICUT. SOON OTHER SCHOOLS FOR DEAF PEOPLE OPENED. THEN IN 1864 GALLAUDET'S SON FOUNDED GALLAUDET UNIVERSITY IN WASHINGTON, D.C.

Chapter 5
Annie Sullivan Arrives

It was March 3, 1887. Helen did not know that this was to be the most important day of her life. Helen was aware that everyone in the family

seemed excited. She could feel the tension in the air. Her mother bustled about the house. Things were cleaned and polished. Her mother and step-brother dressed to go to the train station. Helen pulled her mother, wanting to go out with them, but her mother said no.

Finally, Annie Sullivan arrived in Alabama on the six-thirty train. Mrs. Keller greeted her in a

soft voice, her blue eyes sparkling. A small crowd gathered to see the "Yankee girl who was going to teach the Keller child." Alone in a strange place, Annie looked anxious, pale, and tired.

On the way to the Keller farm, Annie sat in the back of the carriage and looked around her. The small town of Tuscumbia looked like towns in New England. This comforted Annie, and she relaxed. She was eager to meet her new pupil.

Helen stood on the porch. She felt the vibrations of the carriage coming down the lane. She

stretched out her arms for her mother. Instead, a stranger walked into her arms and held her. Helen didn't like strangers. She refused to let Annie kiss her.

But Helen was curious about strangers, too. Helen felt Annie's face, dress, and bag. Then Helen opened Annie's bag. She expected to find the treats that company often brought for her. Her mother tried to stop Helen. Finally, Mrs. Keller had to rip the bag out of Helen's hands.

Helen grew very angry. Her face turned red. She clutched her mother's skirt and began to kick. No one did anything. Then Annie held her small watch against Helen's face. Feeling it ticking, Helen quieted down. The tantrum passed.

Helen followed Annie upstairs to Annie's room. Helen helped Annie remove her hat. Then Helen put the hat on and moved her head from side to side. Annie watched Helen and wondered how she would teach this beautiful young colt of a girl. She was not sure she could. Annie took a deep breath. But tomorrow, she would start trying.

The next morning, Helen was brought to Annie's room. Helen helped Annie unpack. There in Annie's trunk Helen discovered a lovely doll.

The doll was a gift to Helen from the children at the Perkins School. Laura Bridgman, the former deaf and blind student there, had made some of the doll's clothes. Annie spelled the word *doll* slowly into Helen's hand. Helen thought that the doll was now hers. Whenever Helen wanted something, she pointed first to it, then to herself, and nodded. But Annie had no way of knowing this. She was trying to show Helen that *d-o-l-l* meant *doll*—that the word stood for something. Annie took the doll back. She was going to repeat the spelling of *doll* in Helen's hand. But Helen grew furious. She thought Annie was taking the doll back after she'd given it to her.

Annie tried to take Helen's hand. Helen would not let her. Helen began to throw another temper tantrum. Annie tried to sit Helen in a chair. She wanted to calm Helen. She wanted to start the lesson over. No use. Helen got angrier and fought harder. Annie finally let Helen go.

But Annie was not giving up. She ran downstairs and got a slice of cake. She brought it to

Helen. She spelled *c-a-k-e* into Helen's hand while holding the cake under Helen's nose. Helen tried to take the cake. Annie spelled the word *cake* again and patted Helen's hand. This time Helen spelled the word back. Annie gave Helen the cake to eat. Did Helen understand that *c-a-k-e* meant *cake*? No, not really. Helen was just copying Annie. Helen did not know that if she went to Annie and spelled *c-a-k-e* in Annie's hand that Annie would realize that Helen wanted cake.

Once more, Annie spelled the word *doll* into Helen's hand. Helen spelled back *d-o-l*. Annie spelled the last "*l*" and gave Helen the doll. Helen

fled downstairs with the doll. "I did not know that I was spelling a word or even that words existed," Helen later wrote. "I was simply making my fingers go in monkey-like imitation."

Helen refused to have anything to do with Annie for the rest of the day. Annie sighed. Teacher and pupil had a long, hard road ahead of them.

The next few days did not go any easier. Helen stayed away from Annie. Would Annie be able to break down the wall that kept Helen in her silent world? She was not sure.

One day at breakfast, another battle began. Helen always ate from everyone's plate. She helped herself to food as she went around the table. No one in the family tried to stop her nor did anybody say anything. Annie was shocked. Helen was not going to eat from her plate!

Helen flew into a rage when Annie kept her plate away from her. She fell to the floor kicking and screaming. Annie continued to eat. Then Annie asked the Keller family to leave the room. Upset and confused, they left Helen with Annie, who locked the door behind them.

The war was on.

Annie returned to finish her breakfast. Helen tried to knock over Annie's chair. She failed. Helen began to quiet down. Then, she got up and felt around the table. She realized that only Annie was in the room. Helen was confused. She tried again to steal food from Annie's plate, but Annie would not let her. Finally, Helen sat in her place.

Helen began to eat her breakfast with her fingers.

Annie put a spoon in Helen's hand. She threw it to the floor. Annie made Helen pick it up. Then Annie held the spoon in Helen's hand and made her eat with it. Realizing that Annie would not give up, Helen finished her breakfast using the spoon.

Next came the napkin. Annie wanted Helen to fold it. Helen threw the napkin onto the floor. She ran to the door. Finding it locked, Helen began to kick and scream again. Annie spent the following hour getting Helen to fold her napkin. When it was finally folded, Annie let Helen out. Helen ran outside far away from Annie. Worn out, Annie went to her room.

After a good cry, Annie felt better. Annie said of these battles, "To get her to do the simplest things, such as combing her hair or washing hands . . . it was necessary to use force, and of course, a distressing scene followed." The family could not stand these scenes. They tried to help Helen. Her father could not stand to see her cry. Their helping Helen did not allow Annie to teach her. So Annie came to a decision.

Annie realized that she had to live alone with Helen. Just the two of them. It was the only way Annie could break down Helen's dark, silent wall. Annie talked to the Kellers. She thought they'd say no, but they didn't. The Kellers would do anything to help Helen. So Helen and Annie went to stay in the cottage near the big house.

Annie did not want Helen to know that she was only a quick run from the house and her parents. So Annie had all the furniture moved around in the cottage. Then Annie and Helen went on a long ride in the carriage before arriving at the

cottage. It worked. Helen thought she was in a new, strange place.

Helen and Annie had many battles in the cottage. Annie would not let Helen eat until she was dressed. Helen refused to get dressed.

Captain Keller watched through a window one day. He wanted to send Annie away, but the family talked him out of it. And it was lucky that they did.

Over the next two weeks, Helen slowly began to change. She began to obey Annie.

Then on April 5, 1887, a miracle happened. Helen was washing the dishes. Annie spelled the word *water* in her hand. Helen did not react. The two went outside.

At the water pump. Helen held her mug under the tap. Annie pumped out the cold water and spelled *water* in Helen's hand. Helen dropped the mug. A look of wonder filled her face. Helen spelled back *water* several times to Annie. Now, at last, Helen understood that words stood for things!

Later in her autobiography, Helen wrote, "Everything had a name, and each name gave birth to a new thought."

Annie spelled many different words into Helen's eager hands. Finally, Helen asked what to

call Annie. Annie spelled *teacher.* And so Annie became Teacher. At seven, Helen's world had opened at last. The wall had come down. Annie and Helen moved back to the main house.

Helen made rapid progress. Annie saw that Helen loved to be outdoors. So most of their lessons were outside. Annie used the world around them to teach Helen. By the river, Helen learned geography. They dug canals and built mountains. For science, they studied nature. Helen soon knew many different plants and

how they grew. Helen loved words and language.

Helen memorized words easily. She learned nouns, verbs, and descriptive words. She began to understand abstract words, such as *think*. Helen could now "talk" to her family. Annie spelled what people said into Helen's hand. Then Helen replied. Mrs. Keller learned to speak with her fingers. Now she and Helen could talk. Even Captain learned to speak this way.

By June, Helen knew about four hundred words. Annie wrote to Mr. Anagnos. She told him of Helen's progress. Mr. Anagnos told the Boston newspapers about Helen. The papers ran stories about her. Readers wanted to know more about this deaf-blind child who was beautiful and smart.

Most children Helen's age could read and write. Annie decided that Helen would learn to read and write, too. Annie read books to Helen. She did this by spelling out the whole story in Helen's hand. Helen's world became filled with fairy tales, heroes, villains, myths, and legends.

Annie taught Helen to write. She used a wooden writing board that had grooves on it. A paper was placed over the grooves. Helen then guided her pencil to form letters. This is how blind people learn to write.

Helen had made great progress. She learned Braille, too. Braille is a system of writing for the blind. Soon Helen could read Braille books on her own. And so, another world opened for Helen.

Helen's life was much happier now. But she still had a temper. Helen had a name for herself when she lost her temper. She called herself "the Phantom." But her tantrums came less and less often. Helen now liked playing with her little sister, Mildred. Helen's mind was now free to learn and her heart was free to love.

BRAILLE

MANY BLIND PEOPLE READ BY TOUCH INSTEAD OF SIGHT. THEY RUN THEIR FINGERS OVER PAGES THAT ARE PRINTED IN RAISED DOTS. DIFFERENT ARRANGEMENTS OF DOTS STAND FOR DIFFERENT LETTERS. LOUIS BRAILLE INVENTED THIS SPECIAL KIND OF WRITING.

LOUIS BRAILLE WAS BORN IN 1809 IN A SMALL TOWN IN FRANCE. HE BECAME BLIND AT THE AGE OF FOUR. MOST BLIND PEOPLE THEN COULDN'T READ OR WRITE. MANY HAD TO BEG TO MAKE A LIVING. BUT LOUIS WAS LUCKY. HE WENT TO A SCHOOL FOR BLIND BOYS. HE LEARNED TO READ LETTERS THAT WERE MADE BY PRESSING COPPER WIRE INTO A SHEET OF PAPER TO MAKE A RAISED SHAPE. LOUIS COULD READ, BUT HE STILL DID NOT KNOW HOW TO WRITE. THEN, ONE DAY, A SOLDIER CAME TO THE SCHOOL. HE SHOWED

LOUIS BRAILLE

THE STUDENTS
A SYSTEM
CALLED "NIGHT
WRITING." IT
HELPED SOL-
DIERS IN BATTLE
COMMUNICATE
WITH EACH
OTHER IN THE
DARK WITHOUT
HAVING TO TALK.
IT WAS BASED ON
A SERIES OF
RAISED DOTS.
    LOUIS WAS
VERY EXCITED BY
THIS NEW KIND OF
WRITING. HE SAW
HOW USEFUL IT
COULD BE. HE
EXPERIMENTED UNTIL
HE FOUND A SYSTEM
OF USING SIX DOTS.

THE BRAILLE
ALPHABET

BLIND PEOPLE COULD READ IT. AND THEY
COULD ALSO WRITE IT. THEY USED A
STYLUS (A POINTED PEN-LIKE TOOL) TO
MAKE THE DOTS.
    TODAY, BRAILLE HAS BEEN ADAPTED
FOR ALMOST EVERY LANGUAGE AND IS
USED ALL OVER THE WORLD.

Mr. Anagnos asked Annie to write a paper about Helen. At nights when Annie was at her desk writing, Helen sat quietly beside her, writing her own letter to the blind children at Perkins. No one would have believed this quiet scene possible just four months earlier.

Mr. Anagnos shared stories about Helen and Annie. The Boston newspapers ran more stories about them. The papers began calling Helen the

"wonder child."
Readers wanted
to meet her and
know more
about her. Some

doubted if the stories could be
true. Either way, Helen was becoming famous.

Annie and Helen continued their lessons unaware of their growing fame up North. Christmas was coming. It would be the first time that Helen understood the holiday and would be able to take part in it. Helen and Annie read Christmas stories. They made up their own Christmas stories. Helen got caught up in the excitement and joy of the holiday. She loved making gifts and then dropping hints as to what the gifts were. The Keller family had much to be thankful for this holiday. And so did Annie who, at last, had a home.

The new year, 1888, dawned full of hope.

Helen would turn eight. But more important, Helen would leave home that year. Helen wanted to visit Perkins. And Annie was going to take her there. But first, Helen had to prepare for the trip.

Annie and Helen worked even harder at their lessons. Mrs. Keller worried that Helen was pushing herself too hard. Helen was often tired. She talked to Annie, but Annie said that she could not slow Helen down. Helen never wanted to rest. There was too much to learn.

By May 1888, Helen was ready to go. But an amazing thing happened that changed their plans. Helen and Annie were invited to the White House to meet President Grover Cleveland! Like so many other people, the president was amazed by how much Helen could do. Most people

GROVER CLEVELAND

thought that blind people would always be help-
less. Many thought that, just because they could
not see or hear, blind and deaf people were not
smart. Helen proved to the president of the United
States just how wrong that was.

Chapter 6
Years at Perkins

From Washington, D.C., Annie and Helen made their way by train to Boston. At Perkins, Helen met the now middle-aged Laura Bridgman. The meeting was a disappointment, however. Laura thought that Helen was too much of a tomboy. Helen sat on the floor. Laura did not approve of that. When Helen left, she bent to kiss Laura good-bye and stepped on Laura's toes. Laura cried out in pain. Helen felt like a clumsy schoolgirl.

Some people thought that Helen was too loud

and laughed too much. But Annie did not agree. She knew that Helen was full of life. Annie wanted Helen to grab hold of life and not wait quietly for things to happen.

Helen spoke at the Perkins commencement. This was an important event. The Boston newspapers

ran stories about the school and the children who graduated from it. Important and rich people came to this event. The governor of Massachusetts was there. The band played. Ten boys showed how well they could do arithmetic. Then came Helen.

Helen had been sitting patiently on the platform waiting for her turn. She smiled and glowed as she waited. She could feel the crowd's energy. Proudly Helen spelled a poem about birds into Annie's hand. Annie spoke the words as Helen spelled. The audience was spellbound.

When the school closed for the summer, Annie and Helen went to Cape Cod. For the first time, Helen went swimming in the ocean. She loved the

feel of the cold salt water on her face. Cape Cod
was to become Helen's most favorite place.

One day, when Helen was swimming, the
strong waves pulled her under. She fought her way
to the surface, swallowing water as she struggled.
The waves tossed her onto the sand. Helen lay
there in terror, not sure what had happened. Annie
ran to her and hugged and comforted her.

Helen had courage. Two days later, she was

back in the ocean, swimming. Helen had only one question. Who, she wanted to know, had filled the ocean with salt!

After Annie and Helen went home to Alabama, lessons and learning again filled their days.

As time passed, Annie thought about leaving Alabama. The local people stared at Annie and

Helen when they went into town. Annie believed that Helen could learn more by living in the city.

So Annie asked the Kellers to let them both live at Perkins. Reluctantly, they agreed. They knew it was best for Helen.

In October, Annie and Helen returned to Perkins. Helen was not enrolled there. She was a guest. But she dove right into the schoolwork. She studied geography, botany (the study of plants), zoology (the study of animals), and arithmetic. Arithmetic was her least favorite subject.

Helen's time at Perkins passed quickly. Poetry became her passion. One time Helen visited Oliver Wendell Holmes, the great New England writer. Later, she read his poems to the blind children at Perkins. Helen sent him a letter. She told Holmes that she was sorry he had no little children to play with, but that he seemed happy with his many books. She went on to tell him what she was learning and asked if her little sister could meet him

when she visited Helen. Holmes loved her letter. He published it in an important magazine called *The Atlantic Monthly*. After this honor, Helen began to take her writing more seriously.

In the spring of 1890, a teacher named Mary Swift Lamson returned to Perkins from Norway. While in Norway, she had heard about a deaf-blind girl who had learned to speak. Helen seized upon the idea. Learning to speak became Helen's dream. Annie tried to be realistic with Helen, for she did not want her to be disappointed. If a person cannot see people's faces, it is extremely hard—almost impossible—to learn to speak. But Helen would not give up.

Annie did not stand in Helen's way. She found a teacher for Helen. Helen had to touch her teacher's mouth as it moved when she spoke.

Helen had to learn how lips and tongue moved to make words. At the end of the first lesson, Helen could say the letters *i, m, p, q, s,* and *t.* Helen had visions of going home and talking with her family. Helen practiced continually with Annie. But her voice was never clear. It was something that would bother Helen the rest of her life. She felt that not being able to speak clearly made her different.

Now eleven, Helen wrote a story she called "The Frost King." She gave the story to Mr. Anagnos for his birthday. It was a lovely story, full of images and color. It was published in *The Mentor,* the Perkins alumni magazine, in January 1892. People praised the wonderful story.

However, Helen had not created the story. A newspaper printed Helen's story side by side with a story by someone called "The Frost Fairies." Helen's story was exactly the same. Helen was crushed. Annie said that she had never read the story to Helen. No one ever remembered reading

the story to Helen. But a copy of the book was in the house where Annie and Helen had stayed on Cape Cod. Somehow, Helen must have heard the story and forgotten it.

Helen was shattered. She hadn't been trying to trick anyone! She went to the Perkins School to defend herself. She appeared alone before a group of eight teachers and school officers. Half of the group was blind and half was sighted. Alone in a hot, stuffy room without Annie, Helen shook with fear. It was like she was on trial for her life. Later, Helen wrote, "The blood pressed about my thumping heart, and I could scarcely speak. . . ."

The group showed no mercy. Again and again, they kept asking, "Who read you that story?"

Helen could not answer that question. She had no memory of it. In the end, most of the group believed Helen. Mr. Anagnos thought that it had all been a horrible mistake. But he felt he could no longer trust Helen or Annie. Their friendship with Mr. Anagnos ended. Helen's time at Perkins was over. Even worse, Helen was never again sure of her writing. Was she writing from her

heart and mind or repeating something that she had heard? This fear stayed with Helen every time she picked up a pen.

Helen and Annie returned to Alabama. Helen was ill most of that summer. She no longer woke up hungry to learn. Helen retreated into herself. But gradually her spirits grew stronger. Now she had to make a decision. Was her education at an end? Or could she find another school?

Chapter 7
Years in New York

The door of the Perkins School had slammed shut, but another door opened. Annie learned about a new school for deaf children. Two men—Dr. Thomas Humason and John Wright—started the school in 1894 in New York City and it sounded perfect for Helen.

NEW YORK CITY

But how would the Kellers pay for it? Helen's father had fallen on hard times. There was no money to spare. Fortunately, Helen had met many rich people, such as Dr. Bell, John D. Rockefeller, and John Spaulding. Spaulding offered to pay for Helen's schooling. So Annie and Helen left for New York.

They settled into a fine house close to Central Park. At the Wright-Humason School, Helen studied arithmetic (still her least favorite subject), English literature (which she loved), American history, French, and German. She also studied lip-reading and speech.

Helen's fame spread. A reporter from *The New York Times* came to interview her. He thought he would meet a quiet, shy girl. But fifteen-year-old Helen amazed him. Throughout the interview, Helen laughed, joked, and flirted.

Helen and her class visited the Statue of Liberty. She climbed to the top. To Helen, the air at the top smelled cleaner. The smell of the ocean reminded her of Cape Cod. Another time Helen's class went to a dog show at Madison Square Garden. Helen loved it because dogs were her favorite animal.

One trip affected Helen greatly. Annie and Helen went to the Lower East Side. This is where many new immigrants lived. They lived in tiny, crowded apartments in buildings called tenements. As many as ten people lived in one small dark room.

Helen could not see the poverty. But she could feel it. The people's clothes felt rough and ragged as they brushed Helen and Annie in the street.

Helen also smelled the machine oil, the sawdust, the street dirt, and the salted fish. She could tell just how different life here was from hers.

Many famous people lived in New York. At a party, Helen met Mark Twain. Twain had written *The Adventures of Huckleberry Finn* and *Tom Sawyer.*

Twain watched Helen read lips. They talked together at the party. When Helen left, she put violets in his buttonhole. The two became life-long friends.

After school, Helen liked going to Central Park. On winter days, Helen went bobsledding. She took riding lessons. Helen was growing up. She was becoming a beautiful, interesting, young woman.

CENTRAL PARK

Chapter 8
Cambridge Years

In the early 1900s, few women went to college.
And no deaf-blind woman had ever completed
college. But Helen was determined to be the first.
And she knew just where she wanted to go:
Radcliffe. It was the sister school of Harvard
University, just outside Boston. Radcliffe was
considered the top women's college in the United
States. It would be an amazing accomplishment for
Helen to become a student there.

Helen learned of a way that she could gain
admittance to Radcliffe. There was a school, the
Cambridge School for Young Ladies, that prepared
young women for Radcliffe.

Annie went to see Arthur Gilman, the head of
the Cambridge School. She pleaded with him to
take Helen as a student. Surprised by the request,
he said that he would think it over. Helen and

Annie had no choice but to wait. His answer would determine Helen's future.

It was during this time that Helen's father died. Helen wanted to rush home for the Captain's funeral, but her mother wouldn't permit it. It was summer when many contagious diseases thrived in the South. Helen's mother did not want to risk Helen's health. So Helen had to stay in Massachusetts and grieve for the Captain.

Then, at last, Gilman gave his answer. Helen was accepted! For the first time, Helen felt afraid of going to school. What if she did not do as well as the other girls? What if she failed?

At first Helen seemed like any other student at the school. She and Annie lived in Howells House, one of the dorms. Helen made friends. Some of the girls learned the manual alphabet so they could talk to Helen. She joined them in games and took long walks with them. Helen studied English, history, Latin, and German.

But few of the text books were in Braille. Annie had to read each one to her. Annie also had to look up words Helen did not know, even if the words were in German or French.

Helen worked very hard. She studied day and night. Helen wanted to finish school in three

years. Was she working too hard? Most students spent five years at Mr. Gilman's school. Stubborn as always, Helen refused to back down.

The constant studying took its toll. Helen became ill. Her sister, Mildred, now also attended the school. Mildred noticed that Helen seemed weak and was always tired. Mrs. Keller became alarmed. Was Annie pushing her daughter too hard?

Mrs. Keller met with friends of Helen's. Should she take Helen away from Annie? Mr. Gilman thought so. Helen and Annie had been together for almost ten years. Wherever Helen went, Annie did, too. Perhaps it was time for Helen to make a break with Teacher. Helen did not want Teacher to leave. Helen felt she would be lost without Teacher.

Mrs. Keller wavered. She was not sure. In the end, Mrs. Keller sided with Annie. Helen would remain with Annie. Helen withdrew from Mr. Gilman's school. She and Annie went to live in

Wrentham, Massachusetts. There Helen worked with a private tutor. Nothing would stop Helen from entering Radcliffe.

In June 1899, Helen took the tests for Radcliffe. She was already nineteen years old. Many freshmen at Radcliffe were only eighteen. Helen was afraid that she had failed.

But she passed with good marks.

Finally on July 4, 1899, the acceptance letter came. The fireworks for the holidays seemed to be just for Helen. But the dean of Radcliffe suggested that Helen wait a year before entering. To Helen that seemed like forever. In September 1900, Helen entered Radcliffe as a freshman. "In the wonderland of Mind," Helen said, "I should be as free as another." Helen's dream had come true.

Chapter 9
College Years

So Helen began her college years. As hard as the Cambridge School had been, Radcliffe seemed impossible. There was never enough time. Annie spelled lectures into Helen's hand. Annie read the textbooks to Helen. It seemed as though they were on a treadmill. There was no time for rest or Helen would fall behind.

And Helen felt alone. She and Annie lived in a small house off campus. It was away from the girls in Helen's classes. The girls were friendly, but many did not know what to say or how to act around Helen. Others felt odd because Helen was famous. So with a quick handshake, the girls ran off.

And Helen was always working. She had no time to play, think, or daydream. She always had a paper due, a lecture to memorize, or a test to take. Helen's first year at college was hard and lonely.

In her second year, Helen began to write themes. The themes were stories of her life.

An editor at the magazine *Ladies' Home Journal* heard about the themes. He asked Helen if the magazine could publish them. He offered Helen the sum of $3,000! Helen was amazed. That was a lot of money. Helen agreed. And so she began "The Story of My Life."

Each month the magazine published a new chapter in Helen's story. The first one went fine. But Helen handed in the second chapter late. The story was much too long. Neither Helen nor Annie knew how to edit. What were they to do?

JOHN MACY

Friends told them about a fine editor named John Macy. John helped Helen edit the articles. The magazine loved the pieces, and so did the public. By the time the last "chapter" appeared in the August issue, the world was in love with Helen Keller.

The Story of My Life
BY Helen Keller

John Macy thought that Helen's stories could be made into a book. John added Helen's childhood letters and a section describing how Annie taught Helen.

Helen's book, *The Story of My Life,* became a hit. It is still in print today. It has been published in more than fifty languages. Now Helen had a career as a writer. No one could ever say that this was not her story. It was *her* life!

In June 1904, Helen Keller graduated with honors from Radcliffe. Newspapers around the world reported the event. Helen had achieved what no other person with her handicaps had ever done. Now she had a college degree but what was she going to do with it?

Annie also had big questions to decide. She and John Macy had fallen in love. He wanted to marry her. But what, Annie wondered, would happen to Helen? Could she lead a more independent life? Annie wanted to marry John Macy, and so they did in 1905. Helen lived with them.

As for Helen, she kept on with her life, too. She published a second book, *The World I Live In.* It came out in 1908 and told of Helen's world. It described how she used her senses of touch, smell, and taste to make up for her two missing ones. The book also revealed Helen's wonderful imagination ad how she pictured her world. The book was a hit. But Helen wanted to support herself. The money from the book was not enough to do that.

How else could Helen make a living?

Chapter 10
All Grown Up

Helen was asked to give a public speech. Helen gave her first speech in Montclair, New Jersey. Annie was with her. Still, Helen was scared. What if no one understood her? Helen spoke about her life. Her voice was not clear, but no one seemed to care. The audience loved her. Helen was asked to give more speeches.

So Helen and Annie went on a lecture tour. They toured different cities in the United States in 1913. She spoke about her life and her feelings and how she accomplished what she did. Annie introduced Helen and then spoke again at the end. Warm and heartfelt applause greeted Helen wherever she went.

Helen was so successful on stage that some people invited her to make a movie about her life and her feelings. Helen and Annie went to Hollywood and made the silent film *Deliverance.* Annie and Helen dreamed of the money they'd make from the film. They hoped to become rich and famous like movie stars. But the movie was not a success.

Disappointed, Helen and Annie returned to Wrentham. And now they had a new problem. Annie's eyesight was failing. And Annie and John had separated. Annie was hurt over the failure of her marriage. And she feared she would go blind. The two rested. Helen answered the many letters that she received. Helen was famous, but they were broke. Helen had to think of a way to earn money. Then an offer came.

New York vaudeville agents met with Helen and Annie. Vaudeville was a stage show made up of a series of different acts. The agents discussed whether the two women might do a twenty-minute act about Helen and her teacher. Annie and Helen's friends did not like the idea. Helen's mother hated the idea. People would come just to see a blind and deaf woman. But Helen didn't care. She thought that it would be fun. And, as always, once Helen decided to do something, there was no changing her mind.

The first performance was on February 24, 1920, at the Palace Theater in New York City. Teacher opened the act. In her Irish brogue, she told how she had first taught Helen. Music then filled the theater. Helen parted the curtains and walked on stage. Then they told of the "miracle," the day when Annie spelled the word *water* and Helen realized what it meant.

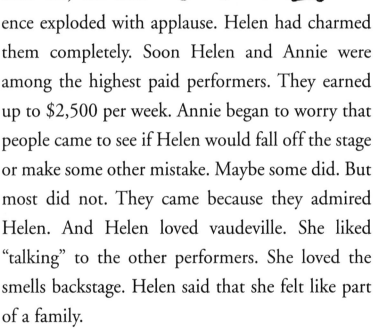

At the end of their act, the audience exploded with applause. Helen had charmed them completely. Soon Helen and Annie were among the highest paid performers. They earned up to $2,500 per week. Annie began to worry that people came to see if Helen would fall off the stage or make some other mistake. Maybe some did. But most did not. They came because they admired Helen. And Helen loved vaudeville. She liked "talking" to the other performers. She loved the smells backstage. Helen said that she felt like part of a family.

In 1924, Helen started a new job, one that was to last the rest of her life. The American Foundation for the Blind asked Helen to work for

them. She would meet people, talk about the blind, and raise funds. Helen accepted. She felt that here was a way to help the blind everywhere. And so Helen became the ambassador for the blind. She met kings, queens, and presidents. Annie went with her.

In 1925, Helen took a year off to write another book. Helen had been asked to write about the most recent years of her life. She wrote about her last years at Radcliffe, the Foundation for the Blind, and the people in her life.

In 1929, *Midstream* was published. It, too, became a best-seller.

Nineteen twenty-nine was also the year that the stock market crashed. The Great Depression began. Millions of people in the United States lost their jobs and their money.

Annie became ill. Her sight grew worse and worse. Later, she lost her sight. Helen's heart broke for Teacher. She made sure that Teacher was well taken care of. A secretary named Polly Thomson began to fill in for Annie.

Then, in 1936, Annie Sullivan died. For nearly fifty years, Teacher had been the center of Helen's life. Could Helen live without her? Many people thought Helen would collapse or fade away. But she didn't. In her heart, Helen knew that she had to go on. She could not retreat from the world.

Teacher never would have wanted that.

So Helen kept on working with just Polly's help. Helen continued to speak for the Foundation. She met with President Franklin D. Roosevelt, who had had polio. He had braces on his legs and used a wheelchair. The two proved that people could overcome severe handicaps and achieve great things. Helen worked to pass laws to help the blind. The blind would receive money for school and job training. Funds were given to make talking books available in public libraries. These laws helped the blind live independently.

Helen toured Japan in the late 1930s. The Japanese people knew of Helen Keller, but many did not believe the stories about her. In Japan, the blind were treated very poorly. They received little schooling or help from the government. Helen's tour changed that. Knowing that Helen loved dogs, the Japanese people gave her a beautiful

HELEN WITH PRESIDENT ROOSEVELT

FRANKLIN DELANO ROOSEVELT

FRANKLIN DELANO ROOSEVELT WAS THE 32ND PRESIDENT OF THE UNITED STATES. WHEN HE WAS 39 YEARS OLD, HE CAME DOWN WITH POLIO. HE WAS NEVER ABLE TO WALK AGAIN WITHOUT THE AID OF LEG BRACES AND CRUTCHES. BUT HIS HANDICAP DID NOT STOP HIM FROM BEING ONE OF THE GREATEST PRESIDENTS. HE TOOK OFFICE DURING THE GREAT DEPRESSION AND STARTED MANY GOVERNMENT PROGRAMS THAT PUT JOBLESS PEOPLE BACK TO WORK. HE ALSO LED THE COUNTRY DURING THE SECOND WORLD WAR. THROUGH HIS RADIO APPEAR-ANCES, KNOWN AS "FIRESIDE CHATS," PRESIDENT ROOSEVELT GAVE HOPE TO AMERICANS IN TIMES OF GREAT PERIL AND UNCERTAINTY. HE DIED IN 1945, NEAR THE END OF WWII. HE WAS ELECTED FOUR TIMES AND SERVED LONGER THAN ANY OTHER PRESIDENT.

Akita dog. This gift showed how much they respected her. Helen then returned home.

After World War II ended in 1945, Helen traveled all over the world once more. She met with blind soldiers. Helen inspired them. She gave them hope.

Helen continued to speak out for the handicapped for the rest of her life. She met with every president, from Grover Cleveland to John F. Kennedy.

In 1955, Helen published another book *Teacher: Anne Sullivan Macy.* It was about the life of the person who had, in many ways, given Helen her life.

On Broadway a play called *The Miracle Worker* opened in 1959. It, too, told the story of young Helen and Teacher. Later, the play was made into a popular movie.

Helen died on June 1, 1968. She was nearly eighty-eight. She had inspired millions. Her story continues to inspire us today.

TIMELINE OF HELEN KELLER'S LIFE

1880	Helen Keller is born in Tuscumbia, Alabama on June 27th
1882	Helen loses her sight, hearing, and speech
1887	Annie Sullivan arrives at the Keller home
1888	Helen visits Perkins School
1894	Helen attends Wright-Humason School in New York
1895	Helen attends Cambridge School for Young Ladies
1900	Helen attends Radcliffe
1903	Helen publishes *The Story of My Life*
1904	Helen graduates with honors from Radcliffe
1905	Annie marries John Macy
1914	Helen hires Polly Thomson
1918	Helen stars in the film *Deliverance*
1919	Helen begins touring in vaudeville
1924	Helen begins working for American Foundation for the Blind
1929	Helen writes *Midstream*
1936	Annie dies
1937	Helen and Polly tour Japan
1955	Helen publishes *Teacher: Anne Sullivan Macy*
1968	Helen Keller dies on June 1st

Timeline of the World

Thomas Edison invents the first practical light bulb — **1879**

The first commercially successful bicycle is invented — **1885**

The zipper is invented — **1893**

Walt Disney is born — **1901**

Beatrix Potter publishes *The Tale of Peter Rabbit* — **1902**

A huge earthquake hits San Francisco — **1906**

Henry Ford builds the first Model T — **1908**

The U.S. enters World War I — **1917**

Women win the right to vote in the U.S. — **1920**

The television is invented — **1923**

Charles Lindbergh makes the first nonstop solo flight across the Atlantic Ocean — **1927**

The first movie with sound is released — **1927**

The stock market crashes — **1929**

The Japanese attack Pearl Harbor; U.S. enters World War II — **1941**

Jackie Robinson integrates Major League baseball — **1947**

Elizabeth II becomes queen of England — **1952**

Soviet cosmonaut Yuri Gagarin becomes the first human to orbit Earth — **1961**

Martin Luther King Jr. delivers his historic speech "I Have a Dream" — **1963**

Astronaut Neil Armstrong walks on the moon — **1969**